T0129628

ABBA'S GIRL

WHAT IT MEANS TO BE A DAUGHTER OF THE MOST HIGH GOD

VIVIAN MONROE

BALBOA.
PRESS

A DIVISION OF HAY HOUSE

Scripture quotations marked (NKJV) taken from the New King James Version®. Copyright © 1982 by Thomas Nelson. Used by permission. All rights reserved.

Balboa Press books may be ordered through booksellers or by contacting:

Balboa Press
A Division of Hay House
1663 Liberty Drive
Bloomington, IN 47403
www.balboapress.com
1 (877) 407-4847

Print information available on the last page.

ISBN: 978-1-9822-2704-3 (sc)
ISBN: 978-1-9822-2705-0 (e)

Balboa Press rev. date: 04/26/2019

Contents

DEDICATION

To my husband for always being there and encouraging me in everything I do, for always telling me "you can do it"...

Acknowledgements

My sisters in the Lord, who shared their testimonies of what it means to be an Abba's girl.

Elles Rock for taking the time to read my rough copies and give me honest feedback, and to encourage me to finish.

Preface

While during my favorite time of the day, my early morning time with the Lord, the Holy Spirit dropped these two words down into my spirit...."Abba's Girl".

When I questioned the Father what do You want me to do with this? He told me very clearly, tell others what it means to be an Abba's girl (a Daddy's girl) and how they too can be a highly favored Abba's girl.....and from that came this book... I pray all who read will be blessed.

Inspiration from Ms. Linda Goodpaster my faithful prayer partner and the one who stopped me in my tracks when fear was trying to overcome me. Thank You Ms. Linda, you have always been so good and kind to me, you and Mr. Jack. I love ya'll.

I thought that what Ms. Linda shared here was right on the mark for when we get a glimpse of the Fathers love for His daughters......

"One of the most important truths I have learned by having Jena, my granddaughter and her mother, Jen in my life is; what it means to have a daughter! Having two sons, I did not know how protective a parent is to their daughter. But one day driving to work, I heard these words "you are my daughter". Wow, for the first time I got a glimpse of how God feels about His daughter."

CHAPTER 1

DADDY'S GIRL

Where do I start, except to say I have not always known I was an Abba's girl. In fact, you might say I was one of the wandering sheep of His flock.

I won't make this an auto-biography of my life and start all the way back to the beginning, but I will pick up in the middle somewhere, and maybe throw some of the beginning days in as well.

Suffice it to say, I did not always make the right decisions while growing up or even after the age of 18 where some might argue that I was then an adult.

In fact, I most of the time made the easy decision which was almost always the wrong decision. I did not grow up living my life for the Lord, in fact I was one of those who made fun of "Jesus freaks". Funny, that is how some see me now.

1

I prefer however to be called an "Abba's Girl". That is what my Father calls me. His girl.

How many of you women and girls reading this now ever considered yourself a 'daddy's girl', meaning your earthly father? I did. Especially since I was raised by my daddy. I can remember at times envying those who had mothers to do things with. But later I saw where my daddy was right up there with those other moms.

I recall one time in particular, in elementary school, when I was an angel in a school play. We had these angel wings made of poster-board and glitter, and they were beautiful except for the fact they kept drooping. They would not stand up right. We looked like a bunch of droopy angels.

When I took my wings home and told my daddy the problem, he right away took them, looked them over and got some elastic and fixed them. How proud I was the next day to wear my upright wings. But even more proud that it was my daddy and not one of the others' moms that solved our problem. As small as that may seem to you, it was huge for me.

That image has stayed with me all through my life. An image that said to me, that I could always count on my daddy.

But could I? Would he always be there for me through life?

There was a time that comes to my mind where I felt like he wasn't. I felt like he had abandoned me and turned his back on me. A very crucial time in my life, when I was pregnant and unmarried with my first son.

Did he really turn his back on me? Later my Father God would show me that he didn't. That he in fact was showing me an important lesson. That although I felt he was indestructible, he in fact was not, and one day he would no longer be there, not because he didn't want to be, but because the Lord would call him home. And when that day had come, I would now have to learn to handle the consequences of my choices without him.

I thank the Lord that by the time that happened, I was a born again Christian and could rejoice in the fact that my earthly father was now with the Lord, and that one day I would see him again, and that I had grown up some and was making better choices.

I also thank the Father that He had given me a good husband who could help me through the trials that were to come. You see I haven't yet realized that I am an "Abba's Girl". When I accepted the Lord Jesus into my heart, I immediately became an "Abba's Girl". In the eyes of God our Father, I was at that moment, I am now, and I forever will be 'His little girl'. I just didn't realize exactly what that meant to me yet.

Now as sweet as that story was, let's not be blinded to the fact that there are fathers who are abusive. Not everyone has or had good parents. With a bad image of an earthly parent, it can make it difficult for them to see just how much and how deeply God loves them.

This is why it is even more important that you are an "Abba's Girl". So that you may call on Him, and He will hear you. He will answer you.

Don't let the image of a bad parent steal from you the love that our Abba, our Father in heaven has for you.

Don't let others tell you what you are worth but instead see what God the Father says you are worth.

He gave His only begotten Son, His beloved Son, His darling Son, Jesus to die on a cross for you. Did He deserve to die? No! He knew no sin, did no sin, and in Him was no sin. Yet He took all of our sins upon Himself and was crucified and died for us. He did this out of His love for you and me. He paid the price once and for all, for ALL, so that we can call God the Father, Abba. Romans 8 v 15-16.

How awesome is that? When we decide to make Jesus our Lord and Savior we instantly become children of God. We now have the right to call ourselves, "Abba's Girls'.

Now that my friend is great news.

We will see throughout this book where our earthly lives and our spiritual lives go through some of the same challenges. There will be times when trials will come and you will feel like you are lost.

Just like when I thought my daddy had abandoned me and turned his back on me, I was wrong. I was being deceived. I had listened to someone else tell me that he no longer wanted me around, that I had shamed him.

Instead of trusting him and trusting in his love for me, I chose to believe that person and lived for quite some time estranged from my daddy.

Isn't that what we do to God? Don't we sometimes listen to what the world is saying, listen to the enemy, and just curl up inside ourselves and give in, instead of running to the arms of our loving Father? Instead of going to Him and letting Him show us the way out, we choose to believe the enemy.

This reminds me of another story. The story of the Prodigal son in Luke chapter 15 v 11-32. The Father in this story is actually a picture of Father God. When the son decides to come home, instead of condemnation, his Father sees him way off in the distance, and picks up his robes and takes off running to him. He falls on him and kisses him all over, He is so excited His little lost sheep has decided to come back on his own.

Close your eyes and picture that. Picture God our heavenly Father, the creator of all things, picking up His robes and running to you. What a picture. Now that is one to call up to your memory and reflect on when things are going bad.

God doesn't leave us. He says in fact that He will never leave us nor forsake us. It is we who leave Him. We are the ones who turn our backs on Him and listen to the lies of the enemy, letting him make us feel shame, so that we distance ourselves from our Abba.

But God says, He sees no shame in us when we are in Christ Jesus. He only sees the blood of Jesus, His beloved Son. And that blood can not be accounted for nothing. We have to understand who we are in Him so that we can understand the depth, breath, and length of His love for us.

In one scripture in the bible in Zechariah 2 v 8, it says that His people are the apple of His eye, and someone once told me that when the enemy is persecuting you, it is like he is sticking his finger in God's eye, and that my friend is not going to go over well with Him.

PS 17 v 8...Keep me as the apple of Your eye; Hide me under the shadow of Your wings.... Let me close this first chapter with these scriptures about the Father and the Son.

John 10 v 27-30...."My sheep hear My voice, and I know them and they know Me. And I give them eternal life, and they shall never perish; neither shall anyone snatch them out of My hand. My Father Who has given them to

Me, is greater than all; and no one is able to snatch them out of My Father's Hand. I and My Father are one.".........

When the enemy is trying to attack you, remember what the Father says....and I am paraphrasing here...."get your hands off MY girl!".....

And that my friend is what you call a Daddy's Girl, protected always by her Abba.

CHAPTER 2

ABBA'S GIRL

Who Qualifies to be an Abba's Girl?

WHAT! You ask? We have to qualify to be an Abba's Girl? What must we do? Are there steps to take?

Ok Stop, take a deep breath! The answer is simple. There is no 5 step plan, there are no goals to reach, no work to be done. Most of you reading this are probably already Abba's Girls.

God the Father our Abba tells us that in order to become a child of God, to be able to freely come to Him, there is only one way. Through His Darling Son, Jesus Christ.

John 14 v 6...Jesus said to him. "I am the way, the truth, and the life. No one comes to the Father except through Me..."

John 3 v 16-17...For God so loved the world, that He gave His only begotten Son, that whoever believes in Him should not perish but have everlasting life. For God did not send His Son into the world to condemn the world, but that the world through Him might be saved...

That's it we confess Jesus as our Lord, as the Son of God and believe in our hearts that He died on the cross for our sins and that God the Father raised Him from the dead, and He is now seated at His right hand, making intercession for us, so that we can call Him Abba.

This is the grace of Jesus. This grace is a free gift to us. Only the gift itself was not free. Jesus paid the price for this gift with His life.

So before we go any further in this book, let me take a moment to stop and ask all those reading, have you accepted Jesus as your Lord, and if not would you like to have this intimate relationship with Him so that you too can be called an Abba's Girl?

Then take a moment and pray this prayer from your heart...

Dear Lord Jesus,

Thank You for Your grace and Your forgiveness. Thank You for dying on the cross for my sins. Thank You Father God, that You raised Him up to be seated with You in heaven. Now I ask You Lord Jesus to come into my heart and be the Lord of my life. Thank You Holy Spirit that You dwell in me now, and will guide me from this day forward. Thank You Father God for the privilege of calling myself now an Abba's Girl. Amen.

Now, that we are all Abba's girls, let's see what privileges we have in the kingdom of heaven.

Just like in our earthly lives, we have what we call an inheritance from our parents. Sometimes this can be very significant and sometimes it could just be like passing down a family heirloom.

If there is more than one child then the inheritance is divided up between them usually.

However in the kingdom of God we all have equal access to the same amount of inheritance that never dwindles, never fades away.

Romans 8 v 16-17...The Spirit Himself bears witness with our spirit that we are children of God, and if children, then heirs, heirs of God and joint heirs with Christ....

What sort of inheritance does that include?

1 Pet 1 v 4...to an inheritance incorruptible and undefiled and that does not fade away reserved in heaven for you....

We are sealed with the Holy Spirit of promise, who is the guarantee of our inheritance...(see Ephes.1 v 13-14)

When Jesus died on the cross He died for ALL sins, ALL sicknesses, ALL diseases, and ALL poverty... (read IS 3 v 5)

The word tells us He became poor so that we might become rich..(read 2 Cor 8v9) And why do you think Jesus would even care about our riches?

I believe that it is because it is hard to be a blessing if you have nothing to bless with. I would like to say be weary of those who preach that you should be happy to be poor. That is simply not scriptural. In fact, I love the story about the building of the tabernacle in Exodus, and the people freely gave so much that the artisans and builders had to ask Moses to ask them not to bring any more. They just didn't give, they gave willingly and cheerfully and we all know how God feels about a cheerful giver. He will bless them with more than enough.

John 10 v 10...The thief does not come except to steal, and to kill, and to destroy. I have come that they may have life, and they may have it abundantly....

Sounds to me like the thief, the enemy is the one trying to keep you in lack and bound to poverty.

I tell you this, it is not God's will that His Girl have any lack, in any area of her life.

For even if your earthly Father knows how to give good gifts how much more so your Heavenly Father, your Abba.?

There is no greater love than the love God has for His children. As much as your earthly parents love you, they could never love you like God. They could not and would not ever make a decision to let one child die over another. And that is what God did. He gave His only begotten Son to die in your place. Next time you are questioning His love for you, think about that.

Now here is another earthly story about how being an Abba's girl shows in His favor on you. One day while on FB reading and catching up on friends, I saw this advertisement about a cream to get rid of flabby arms, (ok so some of you have not experienced flabby arms yet) bear with me here. Anyway I read and re-read to make sure I wasn't signing up for any kind of monthly products. I ordered my cream which didn't work by the way for the low price of S&H $4.99, only then 10 days later almost $200. came out of my checking account and when I called and questioned these charges the lady preceded to tell me how I had agreed to this contract and they would be taking this out monthly $200. I assured her they would not, I went to the bank the next morning cancelled the debit card so they could not withdraw any more funds. The bank said I had to pay the first $200, there was nothing they could do. After researching this product and company I found they have 100's of claims against them and everyone said the same thing they had to pay. Well, I came home and said Lord we need to talk. Your word says in Malachi 3 v 11 that You will rebuke the devourer for my sake when I am faithful and trust You with my tithes and offerings. So I am reminding You Lord and saying these people are trying to devour my finances. Thank You Lord I leave this in Your hands.

The next day, every penny of my money was returned, when they were insistent that they would not give it back, and everyone I had talked to who had gone through the same scenario had to pay.

Long story short, don't let the circumstances or the enemy rob you of your Abba's blessings. Just like times you may have had to remind your earthly parent of a promise they made to you, we can come to our Abba and remind Him of His promises to us as children of God. After all we are an Abba's Girl.

So while there are no works you have to do to be an Abba's girl, only to accept Jesus as His Son and Your Savior, there are however benefits. Those benefits are way too many to name, and the best way to know and experience them for yourself is to always stay in His word, and spend time with Him. Just like you cherished the one on one times with your earthly parent, make sure you save time every day to spend with your Abba.

I ask you how many of you would have known to remind Him of the promise to rebuke the devourer for your sake?

Being an Abba's girl can be as wonderful as you allow it to be. This relationship can be as rich and fulfilling as the time you invest in it. A healthy relationship is one where there is substantial quality time spent together.

How do we spend intimate quality time with the Father. By staying in His word, and praying and listening and talking with Him daily.

Don't just be content to call yourself an Abba's girl, really embrace and walk in the fullness of the life your Abba has for you. Before long your girlfriends and family members will want to know what keeps that spring in your step, and that smile on your face.

CHAPTER 3

LIVING UNDER HIS WINGS

As an Abba's girl we can live under divine protection.

How many of us have been told by a parent at sometime when we were small, don't do this or that? While we thought they were just being unreasonable and not wanting us to have fun, they were actually protecting us from harm.

When your parents had to go out and you couldn't go, they would leave you with a responsible babysitter. Sometimes we may have thought we were too old and we didn't need a babysitter, we could take care of ourself.

Again, they were protecting us, they knew best and they were only trying to keep us safe, while they were away from us and we were out from under their covering you might say.

This is where our Abba is the same. We can abide under His wings and be safe. He also gives us the Holy Spirit to dwell in us, so that He can guide us, and keep us on the right path when we seek His wisdom.

But sometimes just like when we were young and immature and lacking in wisdom, we do the same with God. We try to go out on our own, we try to lean on our own understanding and wisdom instead of seeking Him first and then we must suffer the consequences of our actions.

Just like our parents didn't cause our consequences when we misbehaved neither does our Abba. Our disobedience sometimes puts us in position for harm.

When bad things happen, it is not our Abba, our Heavenly Father who causes us hurt and pain. It is either consequences of our actions, or sometimes attacks from the enemy.

When these times come, and they will, where do we run? Who do we run to?

Hopefully, we will run to our Abba, and to His word so that we can rest under His wings of protection.

When we were young we would run to our daddy for protection, to be our champion, our hero. There may have been times where your earthy father had to use Godly wisdom to guide you and teach you, so that you would not make the same mistake again, or so you would understand how to be free of the attacks.

That is how our Abba is. He wants to show us in His word how to be safe and how to recognize the enemy for who he is, a liar. He wants us to know His truth, and let His word set us free, and give us rest.

In PS91 He tells us, he who dwells in the secret place of the Most High, shall abide in the shadow of the Almighty. Where is this secret place? In His word.

In His word, we find our strength, our protection, our hope, our salvation, our peace of mind and our rest.

For me personally, the first thing in the morning before anything else is my time with Him. In His word, in prayer, and sometimes in Holy Communion. Then I feel as though I am covered from head to toe with His divine protection, His Godly wisdom and understanding to get me through the day.

Prov 3 v 5-6...Trust in the Lord with all your heart, and lean not on your own understanding; in all your ways acknowledge Him and He shall direct your paths....

In this world we have to protect ourselves from attacks of the enemy. Jesus tells us we are in this world, but we are not of this world. (John 15v19) He also tells us He has already overcome the world. (John 16 v 33) He has already paid the price at the cross for us to be delivered from pain, sickness, disease, poverty. He has set us free to be at peace and live prosperous, healed, live in abundance. (John 8 v 31-32)

The way we walk in this victory, the way we keep ourselves protected from harm is to rest in that secret place.

We can't always control our circumstances, there is evil in this world but how we walk through the trials is in our hands. We want to walk through with divine protection covering us. We can be at rest even in the midst of our trials.

Our Abba is covering us always with His feathers, we can hide under His wings when we need to. Who or What then is big enough to come against your Abba, Father God? No one, Nothing!

I leave you now with these scriptures to meditate on and to picture in your mind snuggled up underneath God's mighty wing, and let His peace cover you knowing you are protected.

PS 17 v 8...Keep me as the apple of Your eye; hide me under the shadow of Your wings....

PS 57 v 1...Be merciful to me, O God, be merciful to me! For my soul trusts in You; and in the shadow of Your wings I will make my refuge, until these calamities have passed by....

PS 91..He who dwells in the secret place of the Most High (in his word), shall abide under the shadow of the Almighty (under His wings). I will say of the Lord, "He is my refuge and my fortress; My God, in Him I will trust.

Surely He shall deliver you from the snare of the fowler (from traps of the enemy) and from the perilous pestilence (sicknesses and diseases). He shall cover you with His feathers, and under His wings you shall take refuge. His truth (His word) shall be your shield and buckler.

You shall not be afraid of the terror by night, nor of the arrow that flies by day. Nor of the pestilence that walks in darkness, nor of the destruction that lays waste at noon day. (war time)

A thousand may fall at your side, and ten thousand at your right hand, but it shall not come near you. (statistics are subject to change for God's child)

Only with your eyes shall you look and see the reward of the wicked.

Because you have made the Lord, who is my refuge, even the Most High your dwelling place, no evil shall befall you, nor shall any plaque come near your dwelling.

For He shall give His angels charge over you, to keep you in all your ways. In their hands they shall bear you up, lest you dash your foot against a stone.

You shall tread upon the lion and the cobra, the young lion and the serpent you shall trample underfoot. (we are the head not the tail, He has given us the victory) (now God talking to us)

v14-16...Because he has set his love upon Me, therefore I will deliver him.

I will set him on high, because he has known My name. He shall call upon Me and I will answer him.

I will be with him in trouble; I will deliver him and honor him. With long life I will satisfy him and show him My salvation.....

These scriptures show us just how much our Abba loves His Abba's girls. He wants us to walk under His covering, under His divine protection always. How can we make sure we stay under this covering?

How can we live our lives under His wing? Stay in His word.

(Words in parentheses, mine)

CHAPTER 4

LEARNING TO BE AN OBEDIENT DAUGHTER

Did you get into trouble a lot as a child? I guess I did if you count the number of times my granny told me to go pull a switch off the pear tree. Or if you count the stripes I wore on my legs.

But in all my shenanigans, I only once got a spanking from my daddy. When I did, my heart hurt more than the spanking. I never wanted to disappoint my daddy. I was after all a daddy's girl. He was always at work or out and I only got small amounts of time with him, and when I did, I for sure didn't want to be a disappointment.

The next morning I remember him coming in to wake me up before he went to work and to apologize for the spanking and he was crying. Well, if my heart wasn't hurting enough before now it felt as though it was being ripped out of my body. I never wanted to be the source of my daddy's disappointment or hurt ever again. But I know there were times where I was.

Although I never got another spanking from him, I knew when I disobeyed him for I could see the hurt in his eyes.

Now when we fail to be obedient to our Abba, He loves us anyway just like our earthly father. Although He doesn't give us a spanking, what we might get is a correction from the Holy Spirit in our spirit. Whether we choose to listen to that prompting is up to us, but if we do not there will be consequences. You see it is a fact, that to every action is a re-action. We can not blame the Abba for the consequence, we can only blame ourself.

If our earthly father cries and is broken hearted over having to correct us, how much more so our Abba?

Sometimes when I look at the rain pouring down, I think it is God crying over His earth, for all the pain and hurt His creation brings upon themselves.

Oh how it must have broken His heart when at first Adam and Eve dis-obeyed Him, knowing the consequences they had set into motion.

One of the greatest things about being an Abba's girl is feeling the awesome love He has for us. Having the

Holy Spirit to guide us and correct us by speaking what the Father tells Him to speak to us is another bonus. And when the Holy Spirit leads us to do or say something Abba would have us to do, being quick to be obedient is a blessing. I have learned that being quick to be obedient to the Abba and to His word has blessed me beyond my imaginations often times. One of the greatest feelings in the world, is knowing that we have pleased the Father. The way we know is the way He showers His blessings on us and His favor when we walk in obedience to Him.

Some of you reading this have children of your own, and you know how it breaks your heart to have to correct them. The main reason for correcting our children is to keep them safe from harm, from hurt whether it be physical or emotional. When our child is hurting, our hearts are breaking.

Being obedient to the Abba is not about keeping a set of laws, or demands or traditions.

Being obedient to Him is walking in love. Responding to His calling when He asks you to do something. And when God the Father your Abba asks you to do something, it will be covered in love, it will never be an action to bring harm or condemnation on another.

Walking in love in every situation, and toward everyone. Loving our enemies, and blessing those who persecute us. When we walk in this obedience to our Abba, His blessings will overflow in our lives and His peace that only He can give fills our hearts.

Being an obedient Abba's girl is blessing others, and loving others when Abba asks us to, even if we don't really want to at the time.

Don't wait for someone else to do what Abba has asked you to do. Be quick to be obedient to Him and to His word and live the full joy filled abundant life He wants us to have as Abba's girls. Col 3 v 20...Children obey your parents in all things, for this is well pleasing to the Lord...

1 Pet 1 v 22...Since you have purified your souls in obeying the truth through the Spirit in sincere love of the brethren, love one another fervently with a pure heart....

1 John 3 v 23...And this is His commandment that we should believe on the name of His Son Jesus Christ, and love one another, as He gave us commandment...

1 John 4 v 7...Beloved, let us love one another, for love is of God; and everyone who loves is born of God and knows God....

The word has so many lessons written in it that show over and over how those who were obedient to the Lord were blessed whether it was in their health, their finances, their land or their families.

I encourage each one of Abba's girls reading this to take the time to spend with Him each day in His word and see and taste the goodness He has for you.

Let Him speak to you, what He would have you to do. He speaks through His word.

**In fact when He gave me this book to write, I was quick to be obedient about writing it, and even gave myself a deadline to submit to a publisher. But I let other things change my direction and didn't follow through. The Holy Spirit has dealt with me continually about finishing. So now I have decided to be obedient, and finish the task my Abba gave me to do. **

CHAPTER 5

NEW SHOES

How many of us women immediately rush to tell our girlfriends when we come across a good deal, a real bargain?

You know like new shoes that you got for a clearance price, a price that just couldn't be beat. And everyone who complimented you on the shoes, you tell them where they could find them, you recommend the place so that they can share in the same great blessing.

Well, what about our wonderful relationship with our Abba? What about the good news of our Lord and Savior Jesus? What about the free gift of salvation from Him to us?

How many of us rush out to tell our friends and family of this great blessing we have been given? How fast do our feet run to tell the good news of Jesus and His gift of salvation for all?

I know, it is not always easy because people are not always willing to accept this message. I can remember as a Mary Kay sales director one of the hardest lessons for me was to understand that when people said no to what I was selling or to the opportunity I was offering them, they were not saying no to me personally, they were not rejecting me personally, they just did not want what I was selling. Nine times out of ten it was from lack of knowledge on their part about the product or the opportunity and they just didn't want to take the time to hear all the great benefits that I wanted to share with them.

The same is true with us sharing with others about our Lord Jesus. They just lack knowledge or have been given bad information through bad teachings and preachings somewhere along the line.

First of all we don't want to try to sell Jesus to anyone. He is not for sale. We want to share Jesus and His love to everyone and anyone who will receive Him. We are not trying to sell the shoes when we share the gospel, we are wanting to show the love.

I asked the Lord one morning to show me how I could share the gospel with others when so many times folks just didn't seem to want to listen. He told me through the Holy Spirit to recall the story of Johnny Appleseed.

Now there are lots of cute folklore stories about him and how he walked from end to end of the earth planting apple trees everywhere he went.

Here are some more accurate facts about Johnny Appleseed. He was born John Chapman in

1774 in Mass.. His dream was to plant enough apple trees that no one would ever go hungry. While legends paint him as a dreamy vagabond, they say he was actually a very well organized, careful businessman. He began his adventures when he was about 18 yrs old heading west. He carried a leather bag filled with apple seeds he got free from cider mills. Over the years he carefully and strategically planted seeds and grew nurseries of trees everywhere he went. He soon became known as the "apple seed man". Settlers and Indians alike looked forward to his visits and no door was ever closed to him. He was very religious and preached to people along the way and his favorite book was the Bible.

He preferred trading his seeds for used clothing instead of cash, and he would usually give the best of the clothing away to those less fortunate and keep the scraggly ones for himself, which is probably why he was portrayed as a funny looking man.

Johnny Appleseed died in 1845 at the age of 71 of pneumonia, it was said he was never known to of been sick at any other time in his life.

What a story! A story about a man who had a heart for God's people, all of God's people. A man who planted not only seeds for apples to grow to feed people nutritionally, but also seeds from the word of God to feed people spiritually.

I believe the Holy Spirit showed me this so that I could learn to plant seeds from the word, seeds that someone else would come along and water.

He showed me that I could use the story of Johnny Appleseed and how he went about trying to plant the earth with apple trees so that none would go hungry and how God wants us to share His word with the people of the earth so that none would be hungry ever again.

He said don't try to sell them the shoes. Instead share with them the love of Jesus and let the seeds be planted. Just like Johnny Appleseed made it his mission to feed the world, make your mission to plant the seeds of the Lord everyday, everywhere you go, and with everyone you meet and picture all the apple trees coming up along your path. One day He promises the harvest will be great.

Gen 8 v 22..While the earth remains, Seedtime and harvest, cold and heat, winter and summer, and day and night shall not cease.....

God is telling us that if we plant the seed of His word, there will be a harvest just as sure as there is a night and day.

Matt 9 v 37-38...Then He said to His disciples, "the harvest truly is plentiful, but the laborers are few, therefore pray the Lord of the harvest to send out laborers into His harvest...."

Luke 8 v 11...now the parable is this: the seed is the word of God.....

1 Cor 3 v 6....So then neither he who plants is anything, nor he who waters, but God gives the increase.....

IS 55 v 10-11...."For as the rain comes down, and snow from heaven, and do not return there, but water the earth, and make it bring forth and bud, that it may give seed to the sower and bread to the eater, so shall My word be that goes forth from My mouth; It shall not return to Me void, but it shall accomplish what I please, and it shall prosper in the thing for which I sent it....."

As an Abba's girl, let it be our mission to plant our Father's orchards along the paths He leads us each day. Picture in our mind the apple trees beautifully arrayed with their blossoms in their seasons, and their fruits at harvest time. Think of each tree as a person you shared His word with, and the fruits are all the people they shared the word with. Picture in your mind your Heavenly Abba and in all His riches, He gives to you the task of planting His apple orchard.

What a great picture. How proud your Abba is of His daughter out telling the world of His love and about His beloved Son, our Lord and Savior Jesus.

CHAPTER 6

WHEN I FIRST REALIZED I AM AN ABBA'S GIRL

Once as a little girl I can remember running away from home with my cousin and a friend of hers. I was going to be the babysitter for her friends little girl while both of them worked. We were going to be on our own.

I didn't really give much thought to the whole plan, I was just going along with them. I didn't even consider what this would do to my daddy. (I was raised by my daddy) I never even gave that thought any consideration, actually I really didn't think it would matter much or that anyone would miss me, as there were so many others living in the household and receiving his attention I really didn't think he would have time to miss me. What with him working all the time and trying to just get by raising his kids, taking care of his mother and raising his sisters kids and taking care of each of them.

And then, when we got caught and we did get caught, by the police no less, because my daddy did care and he went straight to the police, you see the other two girls were old enough they could legally do as they pleased. Well, when they brought us into the station and called my daddy to come get me, and when he saw me, he started crying, his heart was so broken, I then realized I truly was a Daddy's girl, no matter how many others lived in our house, this man really did love me and cared about what happened to me.

That is how it was when I came to realize that my Father in heaven saw me the same way, as An Abba's Girl.

We can go to church regularly, attend bible studies, teach the word to others, attend School of Ministry, believe whole heartedly in every written word of the Bible and still not realize just who we really are to Him.

I say this because that is where I was in my walk with the Lord, when I myself didn't realize just who I was to Him.

It happened when we had to decided to throw caution to the wind and pick up stakes and move across the US. We sold our property, moved into an RV, and off we went. Well, not that haphazardly, my husband did have a job, we just transferred from one location to the other, but it was a big geographical change. Now for my husband, he was ok with it, as he was raised an Air Force Brat, and then he himself spent about 9 years in the AirForce. So he was used to picking up stakes and moving. For me, not so much, I had pretty much lived just in my hometown for 50 years. I had thousands of friends, worked almost everywhere, could go anywhere and meet up with a friend or acquaintance, until we moved.

WoW, that took some adjusting on my part.

First of all everyone made fun of the way I talked. You know when you lived in La. all your life and pretty much all your relatives are from East TX., you develop a bit of an accent. That didn't bother me though, I knew I would eventually make friends as I pretty much never meet a stranger.

I put in for a job at the same hospital where my husband worked but didn't get hired for some months later. I had a lot of time on my hands, and also was smack dab in the middle of the rainy season (which is pretty much all the time in Oregon) and I was beginning to get cabin fever living in that RV. So I started watching a lot of TV church if you will, a couple people in particular who I give a lot of my thanks to today for helping me get through that depressing period. And then I started writing what I call "God's tid-bits to me". Just sharing with others each day what God had laid on my heart that day through my time with Him. I was really excited to see that the blog was going all around the world and being read.

Now comes the trying times. It was time for me to go for my well woman annual visit, and mammogram like I have been doing for years. But first I had to find a doctor here. Not knowing anyone and so having no one to get a reference from, I just had to pick out of the telephone book basically.

Well, my first thought was this doctor is really on top of things. I had to have this test and then another and then more. All of which she wanted to prescribe this and that for. Well, anyone who knows me knows that I only take vitamin type supplements and tend to steer clear of any medication. I believe the Word when it says by His stripes we WERE healed. (only to be tested later on that)

Not long after my visit, I started my new job, and I began asking about this doctor. The other ladies all told me the same thing, Oh no, you will have to do this test then that, and you will constantly be going back for this or that, and for sure if she sent you to have a mammogram you will have some abnormalities. WOW, I immediately, said I rebuke all of that and I will not have disease of any kind or abnormalities on my body. Well, they all kind of looked at me like I had horns growing out of my head, I'm sure they didn't know just how to take me)

Sure enough a couple days later I get a letter in the mail, telling me to go back to the radiologist for more x-rays. I am like oh no, they weren't kidding.

Well, the tech kept looking at me weird and asked me again why I came back, and I told her, and she gets the radiologist and he asks the same and I tell him the same, and then I told him I was moving so I would be going back through my hometown and I would take his films and go to where I always go so they could compare. He agreed good idea.

However, I didn't go to the branch of our hospital that I normally go to, I went to another location

(which shouldn't have mattered but....) so they only compared the xrays they took that day to the ones I just had in OR.

As we are pulling into our RV site in NC, where we lived for the first year we were there, my doctor from home calls and says, they want you to have a ultrasound/biopsy, so find you a doctor there as soon as you can, but you know when we catch these things this early, you have a good chance of beating it.

I felt like I had been gut punched. I immediately rebuked him and said there is nothing to catch, I will not have disease in my body. I was thinking what the heck is wrong with everyone, trying to speak death over me.

Well, I told my husband, and I prayed that the Lord lead me to a Godly doctor who would have wisdom and could clearly see what was what and that I would not have to wait long for an appointment for me just to have time to worry over this. Then I called my daughter in law and she told me who her family used, and I called, and they had just had a cancellation right before I called and could see me the next morning. (talking about the favor of God).

The next day I called my son back home who is a pastor and asked him to pray for me, and I immediately started crying, and he stopped me and said "Mom, you know what the word says, don't be double minded and listen to the lies of the enemy." Then I called my friend, who I consider one of my most valuable prayer partners, the secretary to my pastor back home, and immediately she says, "Neta I hear fear in you, and God did not give your a spirit of fear, but of peace and of a sound mind. His word says no weapon formed against you shall prosper, she said now it doesn't say it won't form, but it does say it shall not prosper against you." I needed both of them firmly speaking to me to bring me back to what I know the word says. After the doctor appointment I had to wait a couple of weeks for the ultrasound/biopsy appt. The enemy really tried to use this time to tear me down, to weaken me in my faith, to keep fear growing in me. I was constantly fighting and screaming and rebuking the devil. Then the night before my appointment, I was crying out to God, why God? My heart was breaking thinking that He would let this happen to me.

Then as clear as I am talking with you now, God spoke to me, and said, "Daughter why have you not called on your Abba, (Daddy God) why do you keep seeing me as the creator of the universe, and not as your Father who would never let anyone snatch you from His hands?" This is where your peace comes from Abba in this situation. And these scriptures came to my mind. John 10 v 29...."My Father who has given them to Me, is greater than all; and no one is able to snatch them out of My Father's hand.".…

I slept like a baby wrapped in my Father's arms that night completely at peace.

The next day when I went in for my appointment, again the technician is looking like she is confused as to why I am there. She asks me do I know why they sent me for an ultrasound? I tell her the same story. She says, she will be right back. The radiologist comes in with her. He asks me the same, I tell him the same. He just shakes his head and says, they are all only looking at this one film, no other previous films have been sent to compare. He says the chances of you having anything wrong here by looking at this is 99% nothing. He says, he really doesn't understand why this whole thing has gotten this far. He is really upset about it, and says He is so sorry for all the anxiety and worrying this has probably caused me.

I tell him I am not. I told him how God my Father had told me last night that I had nothing to worry about and how I now know my God is not only my God my creator of all things in the universe, but I now know He is my Abba, my Daddy God who will not let anything happen to me. He smiles really big, and says well then I guess it was worth it. He said God is a Good God, and I said yes and He is an Awesome Abba!

What an amazing feeling to realize that God is not just the God of the universe, but He is a loving caring Father who cares what happens to you. Just like when my earthly father cried because I ran away thinking no one would miss me or care. I could see my Abba God crying when I didn't call on Him as Father, when I didn't think He would care enough to stop my fear, to quench all the fiery darts the enemy was slinging at me. Just like my earthly father would have walked through fire for me if needed, my ABBA actually did, when he hung on the cross as the Son of God.

There is so much more to being a Christian. We have to realize exactly who we really are to

Him, and that is an "ABBA's GIRL.

CHAPTER 7

SUITING UP AND ACTING LIKE AN ABBA'S GIRL

While writing this book, my church has started a ladies prayer group, and we have established a set time, and have a room that has been dedicated as our War Room. A room for doing battle in prayer for ourselves and others.

We are learning through a book we are using to pray strategically and purposefully, and with power.

What perfect timing this has been for me. I see first hand other Abba's girls in action. Women from all walks of life that are now daughters of God. I see how amazing our Father is in the fact that He is no respecter of person.

I feel in this prayer room, this War Room if you will the presence of the Holy Spirit when we gather together, and His power explode when we begin to pray. I see in my minds eye, chains dropping off those who are being held captive by addictions, fears, sickness, pain, etc.

I see women who really understand who they are in Christ, that they are Abba's girls and no one or nothing will stand a chance against the power of their Lord working through their prayers.

You may ask, why is this perfect timing for your book? Well, because I would love to see all of you reading this start your own prayer closets, (War Rooms) either at home or corporately with your church sisters. I would love for all of you to recognize just who you are as an Abba's girl, and recognize the power in your prayers.

Also because the enemy is trying to rear his ugly head against one of my children, and in learning how to pray fervent prayers, specifically and purposefully, he will not succeed in his feeble attempt. I will prevail against him by the authority I have over him in the name of Jesus. I will call on my Abba to defend me and mine.

I will not just write a book about being an Abba's girl, I will walk it out. I will walk with my head held high in knowing exactly who my Abba says I am, and in the knowledge of the power He says I have, and I will take my rightful place in His house. I will not stand idly by wringing my hands like a dish rag with worry, but instead I will stand on His truth and lift my hands to Him in praise and thanksgiving for bringing my child through this trial.

I will use the sword (the word of God) and I will demolish this enemy once and for all out of my child's life. His truth will destroy anything that tries to come against me and mine.

Ephes. 6 v 13-18..."therefore take up the whole armor of God, that you may be able to withstand in the evil day, and having done all, to stand. Stand therefore, having girded your waist with truth, having put on the breastplate of righteousness, and having shod your feet with the preparation of the gospel of peace; above all taking the shield of faith with which you will be able to quench all the fiery darts of the wicked one. And take the helmet of salvation, and the sword of the Spirit, which is the word of God; praying always with all prayer and supplication in the Spirit, being watchful to this end with all perseverance and supplication for all the saints...

Now don't read through that too hurriedly take your time and let each piece of the suit be tailor made to fit you perfect so when the time comes to fight, you are ready to send the enemy back to hell where he belongs.

Just because we are Abba's girls does not mean that we do not have to suit up. I'm not talking about our cute little daily outfits, I am talking about suiting up with the truth, with the word of God. Because if we are going to defeat the enemy we will have to know the truth and speak the truth over every area of our lives.

The word is clear about not leaning on our own understanding but first seeking Him and His righteousness, then we will have what it is we need.

Just like when we called out in the night for our earthly father when we were little girls and afraid in the dark, our father came running and quickly would dispel our fears, and reassure us everything was ok, and he would not let any harm come to us. How much more so our Heavenly Father, our Abba wants to do for us. So don't let the enemy keep you in the lies of fear, but instead cry out for your Abba, and I promise you He will come running. He will bring you peace, and strength to fight your enemy through the truth of His word.

I was always told and maybe you were too, that if the devil wasn't bothering you then maybe we need to check whose team we are playing on . That if we are on God's team and doing things for Him, then the enemy will constantly try to attack us, but if we are living like we are playing on the devil's team, then he will be leaving us alone.

Well, my prayer warrior sister, another Abba's girl told me that she would rather think it is because she is hidden in Him, and the enemy can not bother her.

WOW! I agree. This gave me a whole new outlook on what PS 91 means when it says, he who dwells in the secret place of the Most High shall abide under the shadow of the Almighty. We know the secret place is

His word, so if we want to stay hidden in Christ Jesus and out of the enemy's line of fire and protected from the enemy, we need to make sure we STAY IN HIS WORD!

So how does an Abba's girl dress each day? With integrity, with truth, with grace, with purpose, with an armor of the Father's word clothing her from head to toe, and always always with a smile.

CHAPTER 8

A NEW LANGUAGE

Have you ever tried to learn a new language, like spanish, french, etc.?

Well what about when you became an Abba's girl? Yes there is a new language to learn.

Our words are so very important. The word of our Father tells us that our words speak life or death. Prov 18 v 21. He also tells us to choose life over death. Deut. 30 v 19.

Our Father tells us to meditate on what is good and edifying. Phil 4 v 8.

In other words we choose our words wisely. We walk in life speaking good things and believing and meditating on these things. Same as in prayer. When we pray, we pray the solution and not the problem into our situations.

We surround ourselves with positive influences and not those who will bring us down by talking negative all the time.

Sometimes it can be a challenge being an Abba's girl or for any new Christian if they have not been brought up around positive speaking, gentle loving people but instead were brought up around negative speaking people.

I for one was brought up around negative, racist, foul speaking people. Where even the women cursed worse than sailors. So this was a language I was familiar with, this was how I learned to express myself.

After becoming a Christian, one of the first things I wanted to change was my language. I had no desire to talk filthy using curse words. For me this did not happen overnight. God can change you overnight in an instant, but for me this took time.

To be able to change my language I had to surround myself with people who talked the language I wanted to speak. Good things, positive things, loving kind words, not curse words.

I had to separate myself from those who did not speak the language I was wanting to now speak. I had to remove myself from those who used curse words so frequently you think that is the only words they know.

The best way to teach yourself a new language is to be surrounded by those speaking that language you desire and to replace your words with those words until you can become fluent as if it is your native tongue.

I had to use new words to express my feelings, in place of the curse words and negative words I was so accustomed to speaking.

For if I had continued to talk the way I did, always seeing the negative, never seeing the good in others, always using curse words to express my excitement or anger, how then would I ever be able to witness the love of Christ to others? Who would want to listen to me?

Oh I still slip up now and again like if I stump my toe or something, but then I am quick to repent in my heart and with my mouth. Because quite frankly it leaves a nasty taste in my mouth and even worse a nasty impression on whom I am speaking with as to my character.

The best way to learn the language of an Abba's girl is to stay in His word and to fill our thoughts with His love and His kindness to everyone.

His word tells us that "Love never fails" in 1 Cor 13. If we have His love shed abroad in our hearts, then we will not fail either when we are walking out this love.

An Abba's girl should speak positive encouraging words to everyone, and should speak like a lady and not curse like a sailor. After all who wants their Abba to hear them talking ugly?

Now I don't write this to bring condemnation on those who are still trying to learn a new language, I write it to show you how I overcame that spirit of foul language and replaced it with the language of our Lord Jesus.

I know if you are a new Christian, a new daughter of our Abba, that you too desire to please Him in every way and to share that love with others. So let us develop a language of love and kindness so that when we are in a group there is no doubt that we are an Abba's girl.

And now to address that negative speaking part of our language we want to change. When God told us to meditate on those things that were good, this means that when the enemy tries to throw something at us that doesn't belong to us as daughters of Abba, don't stand there with arms wide open to catch, but instead turn your back on what he is saying and meditate on God's word, His truth.

Replace those negative words with positive truth from His word. When the doctor gives you a bad report, don't just accept it and meditate on it, instead look in the Father's word and see what does He say about your health, and meditate on that. When your finances look bleak, don't look at the figures on that page, but instead look into His word and see what does He say about your abundant joy filled life.

You see when God says in His word to put foul speaking words away from you, He is not just talking about filthy language like curse words, He is talking about all kinds of filthy negative, wrong thinking language and curses that do not belong to you as a child of God.

Replace your negative thoughts with His word. This is when He tells us to take all thoughts captive.

When we are going into spiritual war, God tells us not to walk according to our flesh, because it is not our flesh we are warring with.

2 Cor 10 v 3-5....For though we walk in the flesh, we do not war according to the flesh. For the weapons of our warfare are not carnal but mighty in God for pulling down strongholds, casting down arguments and every high thing that exalts itself against the knowledge of God, bringing every thought into captivity to the obedience of Christ...

So you see when we are trying to change our language from a carnal minded to a spirit filled positive language, we need to read this scripture above and know that it is not ourself we are wrestling with but a spirit of foul language that needs to be plucked out by its roots, and cast into the sea. Recognize your enemies and then cast them out in the name of Jesus.

When we begin to think negative or speak negative, stop and remember who we are and remember Who lives within us. And ask the Holy Spirit to guide you and lead you with the right words.

Let us speak with words like in the song of Moses...

Deut. 32 v 2...Let my teaching drop as the rain, my speech distill as the dew, as raindrops on the tender herb, and as showers on the grass.

What a beautiful language the Abba girl speaks.

The word tells us we have what we say. What are we laying claim to for ourselves with our words? Are we claiming health, happiness, prosperity, peace, love? Or are we trying to claim those things that do not belong to us.

I heard this cd of a Christian woman making declarations as to who she was in Christ, and what she has according to His word, and I was so fired up, I decided to listen and re-write a declaration for myself using hers as a model, and to also find the scriptures that would back up each declaration I made. I now use this some mornings to kick start my day. I build myself up in His word I guess you could say.

Chapter 9

HOLY SPIRIT SKIN

Have you ever noticed how some women, no matter their age has this glowing youthful skin? Their faces just seem to always be aglow with youth, freshness, purity?

I think we tend to notice it more especially in women who are older than we are. I call this 'Holy Spirit Skin'.

These women that I know personally with this type skin (who have not had professional work done on their faces) all seem to have the same thing in common.

Their personalties.

They are compassionate, giving, loving, patient, kind, not self seeking, not puffed up in pride, always wants to believe the best in others, are not jealous and most importantly, they are quick to stop gossip, backbiting rumor spreading, in its tracks. And they stop it immediately with prayers.

WOW! Looks like I just wrote the chapter on love in the Bible found in 1 Cor 13.

These scriptures end with LOVE NEVER FAILS. hmmmm. Now there is something to meditate on, something for us all to strive for.

We are always trying to improve our bodies with this diet or this supplement, this special cream or lotion, but if we could just get this deeply rooted into our hearts so that our blood flowing through us can nourish our skin, we too could have this beautiful youthful skin, this glow from the Holy Spirit, this what I call 'Holy Spirit Skin'.

I wish I could bottle this, I would be a millionaire, but the only way to achieve this beautiful skin is to learn to walk in love in every situation, through every trial and to walk in forgiveness, and not just when we want to, but constantly.

I personally know that I am not quite there yet. So I will continue to practice this love walk and grow in His word, and be quick to forgive others (and continue to put a little oil on my face). Because all the creams and lotions and potions out there cannot compare and cannot give this glow to our skin.

Oh we might be able to puff out our wrinkles a little, or cover up a few splotches here and there, even out our coloring, but we cannot get this glow from a bottle.

We must learn to walk in love and forgiveness, gentleness toward others. We must learn to bridle our tongues stopping gossip in its track so that we do not even let it into our hearing, then we can start our own skin developing into this glowing youthful skin.

This is another responsibility of being an Abba's Girl. Walking out His word. Living in His truths. Now please don't mis-understand me, I am not saying or implying you have to do this to keep your salvation or your right standing with God. I am not saying He loves one daughter better than another because she works harder to be good.

NO NO NO....I am saying that as an Abba's Girl, this is another perk. This youthful beautiful glowing skin. But it is a perk that is a result of our actions. It is if you will, a re-action to our actions of how we represent ourselves as Abba's Girls.

It is how we react in situations that are less favorable, how we respond to those in need, how we love those who we may not understand their actions toward us sometimes. It is our daily walk with the Father.

How can we walk with the Father and His Magnificent Glory not shine through on our faces? Now this is a perk I want to have as an Abba's Girl. You see we as Christians have so many perks that are left sitting somewhere because we do not realize what the word says we can have. We have not studied all His promises to us.

I look at this perk like this. When God smiles down on us, it is like rays of His love and His beauty falling down upon our faces, so that we have that Holy Spirit glow on our skin. And when we are walking in love like He tells us to do in His word, I believe His beauty falls upon our face.

Doesn't that just make you want to walk in love and walk around with your face held up to capture all His rays of beauty falling down upon you. Forget laying out in the sun to catch some tanning rays, instead spend your time walking in love and let the Father's beauty rays fall on you.

Remember no matter how skilled a surgeon may be in his work, he can never give you that glow that can only come from the Holy Spirit within you.

As Abba's Girls we could really stand out in a crowd and light up a room if we only would all practice daily to walk in love toward everyone...

1 Cor 13 v 4-9...Love suffers long and is kind, love does not envy, love does not parade itself, is not puffed up; love does not behave rudely, does not seek its

own, is not provoked, thinks no evil; does not rejoice in iniquity, but rejoices in the truth, bears all things, believes all things, hopes all things, endures all things. LOVE NEVER FAILS.....

I am not saying that these women are perfect in their walk as we know there was only one perfect, and that was Jesus. But just like a plant that is watered and fed continuously, it will continue to grow and flourish, but a plant that only gets watered now and again, never gets fed the nutrients it needs to survive will eventually start shriveling up.

How many of us would love to have skin like Sarah, now I am just speculating here, but if kings desired her even in her old age (like right at 100 yrs old) how must she have appeared? I would say beautiful.

Now we know beauty is only skin deep, but Holy Spirit Skin is as deep as it goes. It is what is going on under that top layer of skin that gives us this glow.

We have to as Abba's girls stay in His word, and feed our Spirit daily so that His light will shine and glow through us.

CHAPTER 10

HOW TO GO FROM ABBA'S GIRL TO PRAYER WARRIOR

When I began this book, I had no idea where I would begin. As it has evolved so has my growth as an Abba's girl. Not only as an Abba's girl but also as a prayer warrior.

I told you in one other chapter about our church ladies organizing a prayer group and a War Room for us to do battle in prayer for ourselves and others.

I have learned so much through this prayer group, from the other ladies, from the materials and books we have read on how to pray Fervent prayers. How to pray with authority. How to pray and get answers and receive Victory over our requests.

I thought I knew how to pray. I can say honestly I was lacking in some areas of my prayer life.

I realized through this prayer group that I not only was an Abba's girl but that I was also called to be a mighty prayer warrior.

Now when we think of warriors we think of giant men, suited up in all their armor and ready to go into battle.

But just like David did not give any thought to the size of Goliath, but knew that God was with him and defeated that giant with stones and his armor being the word of God. The spoken word of God carries so much more power than any other weapon.

I dare say these women in this prayer group, in this war room, could stand against any size man in all his armor and not be moved and not be shaken because of that same confidence David had, knowing without a doubt that God is with them and realizing just who they are in Christ Jesus.

No weapon formed against them shall prosper, and no giant is too big for our God. No problem, no sickness, no disease, no pain, no lack of any kind can stand up against our Abba.

Can you see the strength in this woman of God? First she is a daughter of the Most High God. Second she is a mighty warrior of prayer, given all authority by Christ Jesus to ask and to have what she asks for.

The power is not in her physical body, or in her flesh. The power is in the Holy Spirit who lives in her, that same power that raised Jesus from the dead lives in her. Rom 8 v 11.

And as He is so are we in this world. 1 John 4 v 17. Not when we die and go to heaven but now in this world, on this earth.

So as Abba's girls, we must learn to take our stand, to take our rightful places, and to pray with authority, and quench the fiery darts of the enemy, to cast out all the evil spirits that try to exalt themselves against us and our loved ones, and stand in the gap for all those young new daughters of Abba who have not yet realized exactly who they are.

We must train up new believers, new daughters of Abba to be prayer warriors and teach them to recognize who they are in Christ Jesus

An Abba's Girl!

When we pray we must pray the word of God and not the problem.

And this is the confidence we have in Him, that if we ask anything according to His will, He hears us. And if we know that He hears us, whatever we ask, we know that we have the petitions that we have asked of Him.....1 Jhn 5 v 14-15.....

We know that nothing shall separate us from the love of our Father and no one shall snatch us from our Father's hand. Rom 8 v 35-37 and John 10 v 28...

I hope and pray this book will be an eye opener for all those who read it, and that they will pass on to the other ladies, daughters of Abba in their lives and build up a mighty force to be reckoned with.

An army of ABBA'S GIRLS!

Be Blessed and as always......STAY IN HIS WORD!

CHAPTER 11

ABBA TAKES CARE OF HIS GIRLS

While doing what I call my strategic bible reading one morning, (it was actually a challenge from my pastor earlier in the year to read the bible through in one year) and I took the challenge and have been so blessed to hear my Abba talk to me through His word each morning...

Well, back to what I was saying, while reading in Numbers, I was reading where Moses was dividing the inheritance between the sons, but when he came to Zelophehad, the son of Hepher, the son of Gilead, the son of Machir, the son of Manasseh from the families of Manasseh, the son of Joseph, he (Zelophehad) only had daughters, no sons.

His daughters names were Mahlah, Noah, Hoglah, Milcah, and Tirzah. Now they went to Moses, before the priest of Eleazar and asked..'should they not have a possession among their father's brothers? Why should their father's name die out because he had no sons?

So Moses took their petition before God, and God said, 'the daughters have spoken right. You shall surely give them a possession of inheritance from among their father's brothers.'

Now, as I read, I find the names of these daughters over and over. The first time I saw their names was in Chapter 26 v 33, then again in Chapter 27 vs 1-11 when they confronted Moses about their rightful inheritance. This chapter ends telling how the inheritance law will work.

I first thought wow, the first women's rights movement. But then Jesus has made us all equal joint heirs with Him. Amen. Romans 8 v 17.

I tell you this story to show you where our Abba, our Father God was taking care of His daughters even from the beginning. How exciting to know that even while here on this earth, God our Father considered His daughters and knowing there were no sons, no older brothers to care for them until they were married, made sure they would be taken care of.

It must have been pretty important to our Abba, to have these girls mentioned again and again. In fact the Book of Numbers ends with chapter 36 telling again about Zelophehad's daughters and their rights.

I like to think Abba is showing His daughters just how important we are to Him, that He will take care of us and provide for us.

Aren't you glad you can call yourself an "Abba's Girl."?

There are so many exciting stories in the word waiting to give us hope in all areas of our lives. we just have to

STAY IN HIS WORD!

TESTIMONIES
FROM ABBA GIRLS

Testimony from E.Q.

Although I was exposed to the church at a fairly young age (5), I never really got it until I was an adult. My heart was pierced with the Father's pure love at age 38 after 3 failed marriages. I know the Holy Spirit was wooing me for a very long time, but I was rebellious.

My parents divorced when I was only 2 years old and my earthly father had custody of us children. My brothers and I were farmed out, if you will, to foster-like care through to our teen years, as Dad didn't think he could take care of us properly and make a good living to support us and keep us all under the same roof with him. At one time, my oldest brother lived with one family, the other two brothers with another family, and I lived in another home.

While we were not living with our dad, he never neglected to see us and care for our every need. He spent every weekend with us somehow even though he didn't even own a car at that time and lived some 15 miles away from us.

As you can imagine, I was a daddy's girl...being the only girl and the youngest of 4 children, I'll have to say he did tend to spoil me more so than he did my brothers. Therefore, my memories of my earthly father were mostly good ones. While he was surely not perfect, he was there for me and showed me love in the best way he knew how. My dad really had nothing to do with my accepting Christ, but he was an example of a protective, loving presence in my life. I am sure that had bearing on how I was able to receive love from my Abba Father and my desire to please Him.

Early on in my Christian walk, I stepped into the understanding that God, my Father was more than my creator. From the start I was hungry to know Him and received the Baptism of the Holy Spirit soon after my conversion. He spoke to me through the Word and also through music and dance. I loved worshipping Him just dancing all around the living room to praise and worship music, singing my heart out; and luxuriating in His presence. He taught me early on to be a prayer warrior because of circumstances in my life.

Soon after receiving Christ, I had another failed marriage, (this was #3). It was devastating to me to feel like I had failed once again. But in His UNFAILING LOVE, He spoke to me through songs that it was okay and that He would work it out for me. "Count Your Blessings" and "It Will Be Worth it All When We See Jesus." He used the words to both these songs to bring me comfort and release. He continued to speak to my heart and made my crooked ways straight while going through the process of yet another divorce. It was His hand on mine to finally bring us into a place of peace.

My life before Abba was quite chaotic, strewn with all manners of wrong choices, bad decisions, all because I really had no one to turn to; no one I could really trust in the natural to speak of. Or at least, so I thought. Of course, God did put Godly people in my path, but I was so rebellious, I just didn't get it. But I know now that their prayers were so instrumental to my finally submitting myself...all that I am and all that I ever will be...to my precious Abba.

I am so thankful for His total forgiveness; for His protection when I was so foolhardy and headstrong, and didn't even know I needed protecting. I am so thankful for the men and women of God that He placed in my path to mentor me; to help lead me and guide me in moving forward in Christ Jesus.

So now as I look back, I am no longer the person I used to be. I don't even like looking back to be honest, but it's a reminder of how amazing God's transformation truly is.

I am truly a daughter of my Divine Abba Father.

E.Q.'s testimony reminds me of the story of the prodigal son in Luke chapter 15, only in this case we would say the "prodigal daughter". She shares in the beginning how she was exposed to the church some as a child and we can see where scripture holds true in Prov 22 v 6..train up a child in the way he should go, and when he is old he will not depart from it... Now it doesn't

say that we wont stray off the path, what this scripture is telling us is that we can lay a foundation, but it may not be built on until later in God's perfect timing.

Just like the prodigal son, this daughter says she was rebellious, hard headed and chose to step out into the world on her own. Notice she stepped away just like the prodigal son, he left. His Father didn't leave him, no he left his Father. You notice I capitalize Father, because the story is actually about God the Father and we are all prodigals at some time in our lives I dare say.

When just like this son, this daughter saw how much she needed the Father and His love for her, it was then that she submitted to Him, then that she could accept His total forgiveness through His Son Jesus. It was then that she realized how He had super naturally protected her and kept her from harm during her rebellious life style. She could see now more clearly how He did place Godly people in her life, and how the fervent prayers of His people are answered, and how these prayers eventually drew her to Him.

He didn't stop there, He continued to place Godly mentors in her life to help lead her and guide her forward in her walk with Christ Jesus.

He helped her to really see who she was in Christ Jesus. A beloved daughter of God the Father, an "Abba's Girl", resting in the love of Jesus and in the Father's arms.

I will tell you this, she is now a mighty prayer warrior, a devoted daughter of the Father and I would gladly bring my prayer requests to her to stand in agreement with me, for I have seen first hand this mighty woman of God in action in prayer.

Through this book you will have realized that I just don't ask anyone to pray for me, unless I know them and know that they know the word and know how to pray the word and speak the truth, the WORD over my prayer requests, and not pray the problem.

Thank you E.Q. for sharing your testimony and I pray that this will help lead another daughter to the loving arms of the Father. For the word says in Rev. 12 v 11, that we overcome by the Blood of the Lamb, and the word of our testimony.

We are truly sisters, sisters in Christ Jesus, we are a couple of "Abba's Girls."

Testimony from A.H.

I love A H.'s testimony and you will see why as you read it. She is one who truly would have seemed to have had a hard time accepting the love of the Father since she did not have a good role model in her life.

How does someone like AH. who did not feel the love of her natural parents come to believe that a God, someone who she has never seen physically could possibly love her and treat her as His beloved child?

I believe that the reason AH. was able to see the love of God the Father, for her, is because she was brought up going to church and learning the word of God.

Testimony from AH.

One of the greatest lessons I have learned in life is that God knows everything and I do not. God's ways are perfect and mine are not. God is all knowing and therefore knows what is ultimately best for us.

This is easy to forget when facing difficult times but once you remind yourself of this,the situation becomes more manageable.

My childhood was a difficult one. I was born number six of seven children in a family full of turmoil. My parent's relationship was less than the best. My mom had seven children between the ages of newborn to eleven years old. A huge responsibility to say the least. My dad would go missing for long periods of time while constantly cheating on my mother. We would often run out of food and there were plenty of times that my mom would not eat at all from fear of not having enough for the children.

When I was three years old my mom had finally had enough and so she abandoned us all and took up with another man. Suddenly my dad had the responsibility of all of us children. Ultimately he made the decision to place us in a children's home. Thankfully I was too young to have the memories of those days ctched in my mind. Remember I was only three years old.

The home itself was not a horrible place. Although it was more like an institution rather than a home. You were more like a number of many rather than someone's child. All of our basic needs were met.

We had clean clothes and food to eat. However, there were no intimate times such as having a bedtime story read to you.

We were taken to church regularly which I am grateful for. I began learning at an early age about God and His goodness.

Even though my parents had failed miserably I somehow knew that God loved me. For as long as I can remember I was always aware of God and felt His presence in my life. As a young child, however, I didn't understand why things were the way they were.

I always questioned God as to why he didn't just put me with a normal family. Now as an adult I realize that no one's family is "normal" at least not the way I thought of as normal.

Rejection and shame have been the biggest issues I have had to deal with.

Growing up I questioned that if my own parents didn't want me then why would anyone else? You kind of feel like damaged merchandise. You're not quite good enough. You just don't fit in. Even though the feelings are real I have to remind myself that they are lies from Satan himself. He wants me to be stuck in that place of self-doubt because as long as I am, I can't be affective for God.

I remind myself of who God says that I am. He says that I am loved and that He has chosen me. He loves me with an everlasting love. I am His child. He is my father. You can't get any better than that!

AH.

I am reminded of the story of the woman with the issue of blood. She dealt with this illness for 12 years before finally going to the Lord for her healing. Matthew 9 v 20-22. She had spent all her money, used up all her resources to find a cure. She had not met the Lord Jesus, she had only heard of Him and His willingness to heal ALL those who came to Him. Her faith came by hearing, just like AH.'s faith came by hearing the word of God as she was growing up.

Sometimes our healing is not a physical issue with our body but instead an issue with our minds, with our thoughts. AH saw herself as unwanted, as damaged, but God her Father saw her as beautiful and desperately wanted her to be His own daughter. So much so He sent His only begotten Son to die on a cross for her so that she could be called His daughter. AH trusted the Lord to be who He said He was and to love her like He said He would. Unconditionally.

There are many of us who go through life growing up without that nurturing touch from a loving parent, but I thank the Lord that someone took the time to tell us about Jesus and His love for us. No matter how filthy or unappreciated we have been made to feel, the love of the Father for us is greater than any love from any one on this earth, and all He sees in us when we are in Christ Jesus is beauty.

1 Pet 3 v 3-4... Do not let your adornment be merely outward, arranging the hair, wearing gold, or putting on fine apparel, rather let it be the hidden person of the heart, with the incorruptible beauty of a gentle and quiet spirit, which is very precious in the sight of God....

That is my description of an Abba's girl.

You know when it comes to being an Abba's girl we all have this in common, we are all adopted daughters of God.

Thank you AH for sharing with us your testimony. AH is for certain an Abba's Girl.

My Life as an Abba's Girl...

1. When did I become a child of God?

My Life as an Abba's **Girl. ..**

2. When did I realize I was an Abba's **Girl,** and what it meant to have a Father/Daughter relationship, not just a Creator God relationship?

My Life as an Abba's **Girl**

3. How did my relationship with my earthly father help me or not to have a Father daughter relationship with God?

My life as an Abba's **Girl**

4. What is one incident **in** my life that I could compare to a biblical story of what it means to be an Abba's **girl**

My life as an Abba's **Girl**

5. How has being an Abba's **girl** changed my life? What was my life like before realizing I was an Abba's **girl?**

My life as an Abba's girl

6. How can I grow from this day forward as an Abba's girl and in my walk with the Father?

ABOUT THE AUTHOR

Vivian Monroe (better known as Neta) and that is pronounced Nita.

Born and raised in Shreveport, La. She lived in Shreveport for more than 50 years, before moving to NC with her husband Rob for a job transfer.

She has two sons. Her oldest son Brandon Mitchell and his lovely wife Emily (who Neta says is her daughter in love) resides in Shreveport,La. She is the proud nonni of one grandson Eli Mitchell.

Her younger son Joshua Mitchell and future daughter in love, Jenny live in NC. She and Rob lived in Shreveport, La. and for the past 12 years in Salisbury, NC.

Her home church is in Shreveport, La Word of Life Center with Pastors Sam and Becky Carr, where she says she really came to know the word through Pastor Sam's teaching.

This is her first book of what she hopes will be more. She began writing about 11 years ago, writing a column she calls "God's tid-bits to me". She started writing these each day after she would spend time in the word with the father. She first was sending by email to her friends and family members, then co-workers, then more and more people were asking to be put on the list to receive God's tid-bits.

Later after moving to Salisbury, she met a new friend, Michelle, who introduced her to writing a column for the newspaper there. So after writing for about two years articles to be published in the Faith section of the local newspaper on Saturdays, she decided it was time to write her book.

She fully intended on the first book being a devotional with some of her past tid-bits, but God had a different plan.

He gave her the words "Abba's Girls". When she asked what he wanted her to do with these words, she felt Him leading her to write a book about how much He loves ALL His daughters.

She plans to write those tid-bit devotionals as well one day, along with another book that is coming to light as she brings this one forth.

Neta is passionate about staying in His word daily, and always ends her tid-bits with "Stay In His Word!" Now she would like to end this book the same way...

STAY IN HIS WORD!

Printed in the United States
By Bookmasters